D0934471

DISCARDED:
OUTDATED, REDUNDANT
MATERIAL

THE ROCK

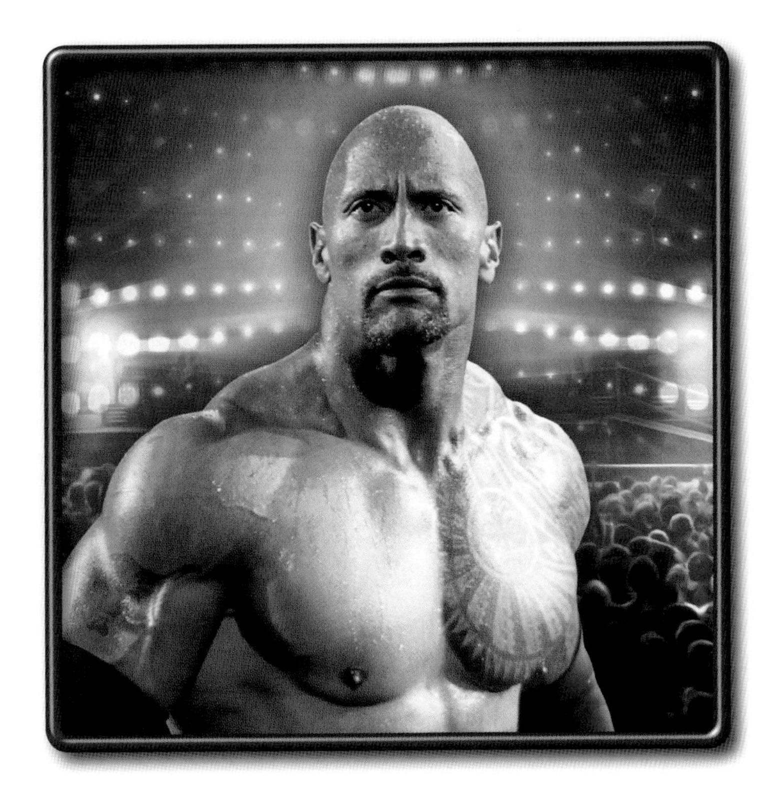

by Michael Sandler

Consultant: Eric Cohen
Wrestling Expert
prowrestling.about.com

New York, New York

Credits

Cover and Title Page, © Picture Perfect/Rex USA/BEImages; TOC, © Chris Ryan/Corbis; 4, © Picture Perfect/Rex USA/BEImages; 5, © Picture Perfect/Rex USA/BEImages; 6, © Mike Fox/ZUMA Press/Newscom; 7, © Rob Kim/Getty Images; 8, © Jeff Steinberg/Pacific Coast News/Newscom; 9, © Abdol Malek Muhammad Imran; 10, © US PRESSWIRE; 11, © Miami/Collegiate Images/Getty Images; 12, © Matt Roberts/ZUMA Press/Newscom; 13, © UPN/Courtesy Everett Collection; 14, © Walt Disney Co./Courtesy Everett Collection; 15, © Warner Bros. Pictures/Courtesy Everett Collection; 16, © Kevin Mazur/WireImage/Getty Images; 17, © Joe Stevens/Retna Ltd.; 18, © Carrie Devorah/WENN.com/Newscom; 19, © Joe Stevens/Retna Ltd.; 20, © Matt Roberts/ZUMA Press/Alamy; 21, © Jason DeCrow/AP Images for Nickelodeon; 22T, © Duomo/Corbis; 22B, © Ron Elkman/Sports Imagery/Getty Images.

Publisher: Kenn Goin
Senior Editor: Lisa Wiseman
Creative Director: Spencer Brinker
Photo Researcher: We Research Pictures, LLC
Design: Debrah Kaiser

Library of Congress Cataloging-in-Publication Data

Sandler, Michael, 1965–
The Rock / by Michael Sandler ; consultant, Eric Cohen.
p. cm. — (Wrestling's tough guys)
Includes bibliographical references and index.
ISBN 978-1-61772-574-6 (library binding) — ISBN 1-61772-574-9 (library binding)
1. Johnson, Dwayne, 1972- 2. Wrestlers—United States—Biography—Juvenile literature. 3. Actors—United States—Biography—Juvenile literature. I. Title.
GV1196.J64S26 2013
796.812092—dc23
[B]

2012014766

For more information, write to Bearport Publishing Company, Inc., 45 West 21st Street, Suite 3B, New York, New York 10010. Printed in the United States of America.

10 9 8 7 6 5 4 3 2 1

Contents

The Rock's Return

In 2004, The Rock was pro wrestling's biggest superstar. Then he left the **WWE** to become an actor. Seven years later, on November 20, 2011, he returned to the ring. For his return, The Rock joined 12-time World Champion John Cena for one of history's greatest **tag team** matches.

The Rock

From 1996 to 2004, The Rock was one of the WWE's greatest wrestlers. During that time, he won nearly every major WWE title.

To defeat the powerful **opposing duo**—The Miz and R-Truth—The Rock would need to rely on his old wrestling skills. Did he still have the power, **technique**, and **fury** that had once made him a champion? The world was about to find out!

John Cena (left) and The Rock (right) in the ring

On the Move

As a child, The Rock was known by his real name, Dwayne Johnson. Dwayne was born on May 2, 1972, in Hayward, California. However, he didn't live there for very long.

Hayward is a city of more than 140,000 people. It is located in Northern California.

Dwayne's father, Rocky Johnson, was a pro wrestler. To earn a living, Rocky had to move from place to place. He wrestled in different areas of the country, taking his family with him. By the time Dwayne started kindergarten, he had already lived in five different states.

Rocky Johnson in 2011

Rocky Johnson wasn't the only pro wrestler in Dwayne's family. Dwayne's grandfather Peter Maivia had also been a wrestling champion in the 1960s and 1970s.

Just Like Dad

Dwayne didn't mind moving around all the time. He loved the fact that his father was a wrestler. He thought it was exciting to go to his dad's matches and cheer wildly for him.

The Rock shows off his muscles in 2012

When Dwayne was a teen, he worked out with weights to become big and strong like his dad. At 15 years old, he already stood well over six feet (1.83 m) tall and weighed 225 pounds (102 kg).

Often, Dwayne tried to copy his dad's wrestling moves. Most of all, however, he loved playing with his father's championship belts. Dwayne would hold them up high in the air, pretending to be a pro wrestler who'd just won a match. There was nothing Dwayne wanted more than to grow up and become a wrestler like his dad. He certainly had the size and strength to do so. He was usually the biggest kid in his class.

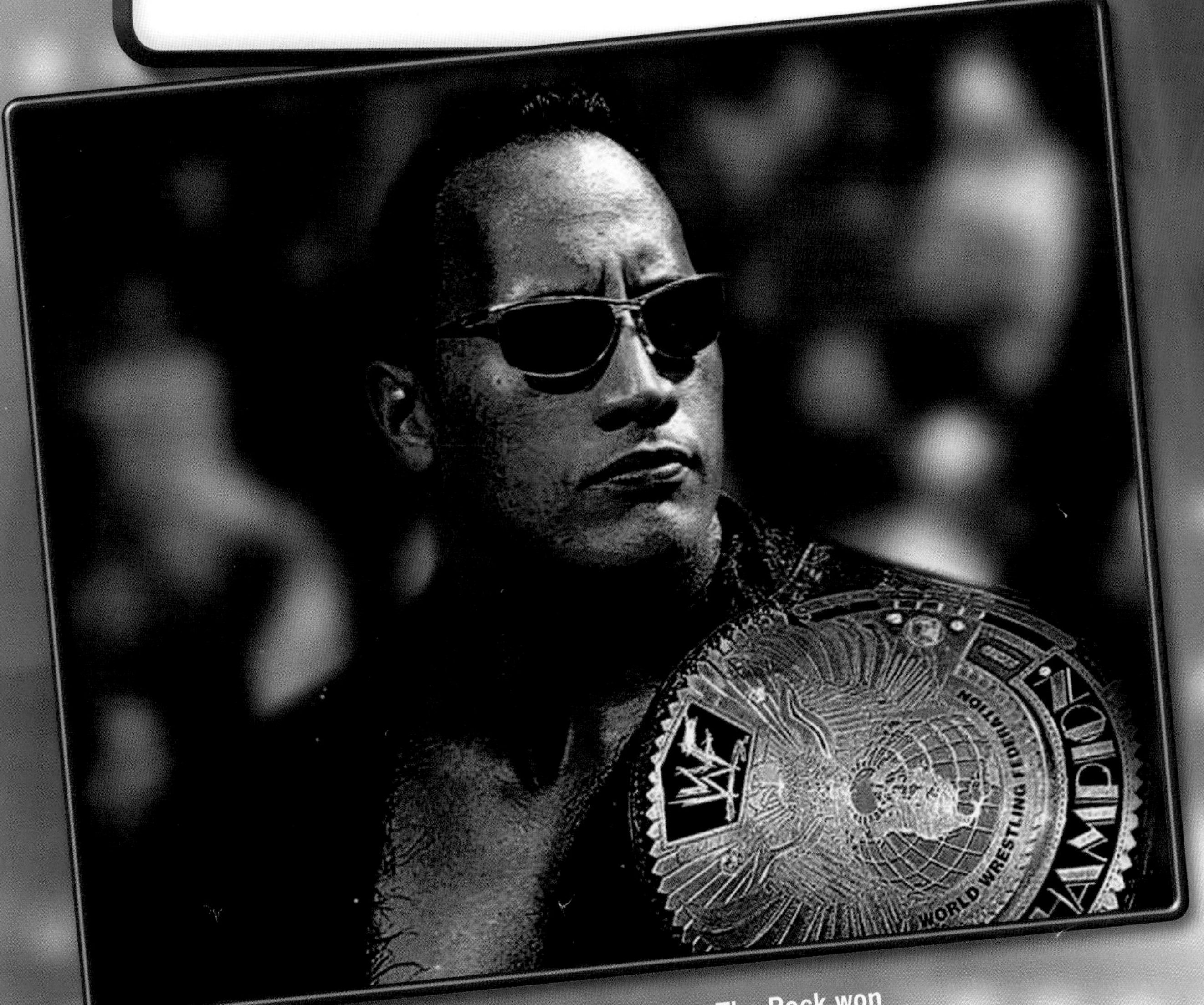

After becoming a wrestler, The Rock won championship belts—just like his dad.

Becoming a Wrestler

Strong and muscular like his father, Dwayne became a star football player in high school and college. He even went on to play in the **Canadian Football League**.

Dwayne played college football for the University of Miami Hurricanes.

Unfortunately, injuries ended Dwayne's football career. So he turned his attention to his childhood dream—wrestling. At age 23, he told his father, "I just feel like this is what I was born to do." His father agreed to train him and show Dwayne everything he knew. Soon Dwayne was wrestling as a professional. In 1996, Dwayne joined the WWE, the biggest and most popular wrestling group in the United States.

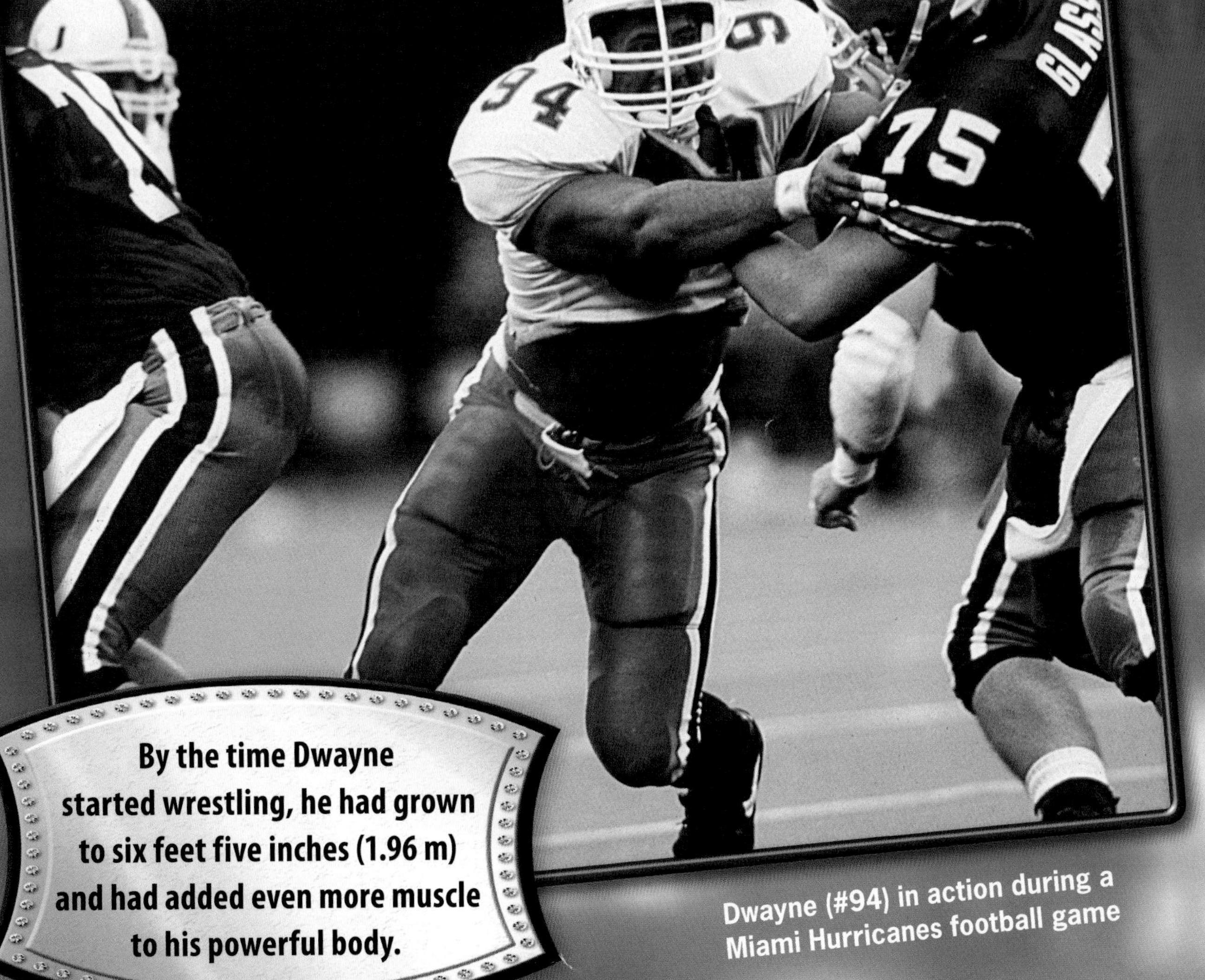

By the time Dwayne started wrestling, he had grown to six feet five inches (1.96 m) and had added even more muscle to his powerful body.

Dwayne (#94) in action during a Miami Hurricanes football game

Superstar

Dwayne quickly became one of the organization's top wrestlers. Just three months after joining the WWE, he won the **Intercontinental Championship** from Triple H.

Triple H

Dwayne began his VWE career using the name ›cky Maivia—a combination ıis father's and grandfather's ng names. Soon he became ›own by a shorter and simpler name—The Rock.

Then, less than two years later, he battled for the **WWE Championship**, facing the **villainous** wrestler Mankind. For much of the match, each wrestler held his own, battling fiercely against the other. Then The Rock caught Mankind in a **Sharpshooter**, twisting his opponent like a pretzel. The move caused Mankind to scream and the match ended. The Rock had just won the biggest title in pro wrestling. Now he was the WWE's most **dominant** wrestler.

Mankind

Moving into the Movies

By 2004, The Rock had won the WWE Championship seven times. Then, surprisingly, the world's most exciting wrestler decided to step away from the sport that had made him famous. The Rock decided it was time to fulfill another dream—to become a full-time actor.

When acting in television shows or in movies, The Rock goes by his real name—Dwayne Johnson. In 2009, Dwayne starred in the movie *Race to Witch Mountain*.

Dwayne has appeared in more than 15 films, from *The Mummy Returns* (2001) to *Race to Witch Mountain* (2009). His first starring role came in 2001 with the movie *The Scorpion King*.

In 1999, The Rock had begun to act, earning small **roles** on television shows. Soon, however, Dwayne won bigger parts and, in 2004, gave up wrestling to focus on his acting career. He became extraordinarily popular—an even bigger superstar than he had been in the ring. Despite his film success, wrestling fans missed watching him in action. That's why they were so excited when The Rock decided to return to wrestling in November 2011.

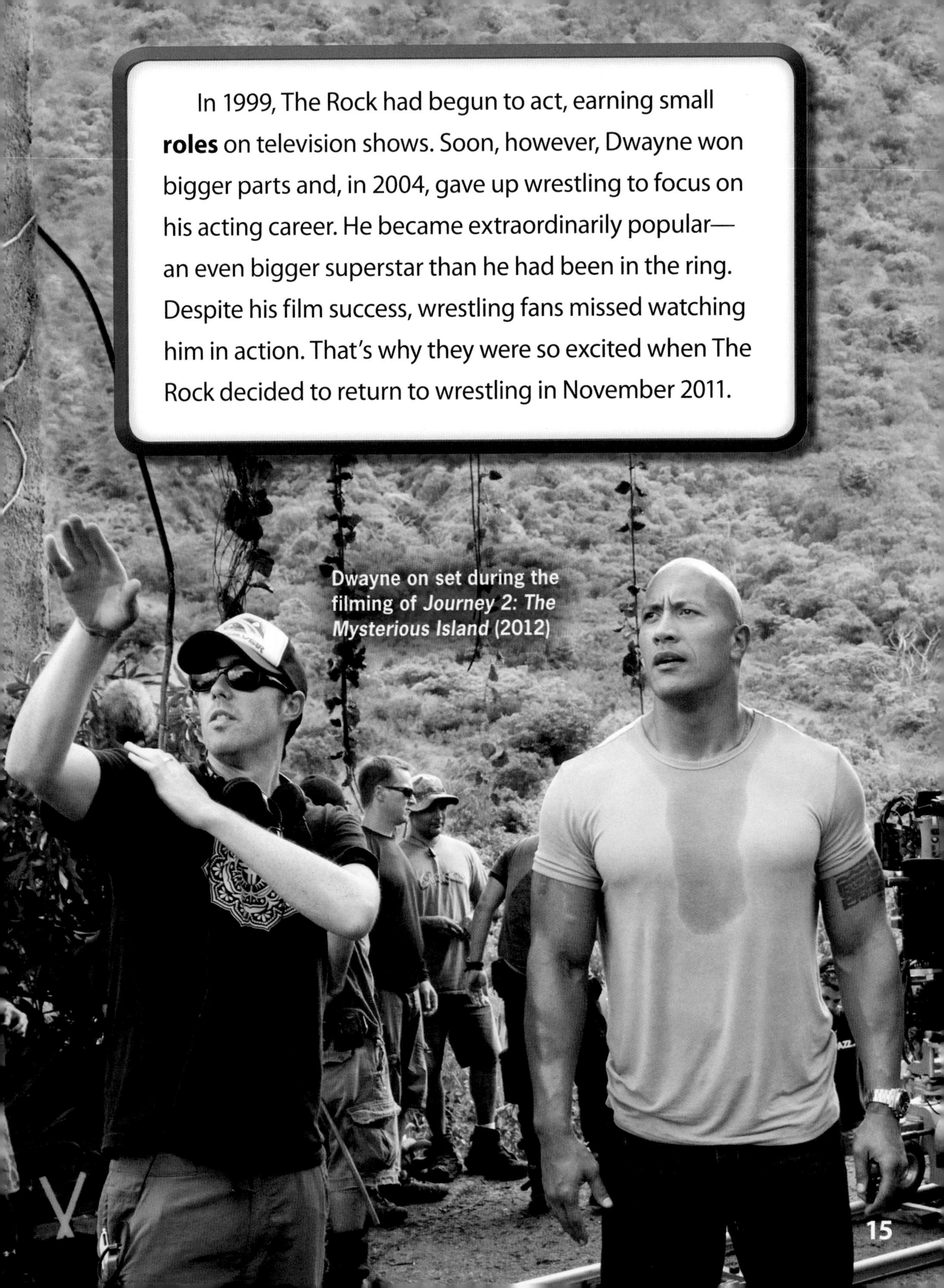

Dwayne on set during the filming of *Journey 2: The Mysterious Island* (2012)

Back in the Ring

The day of The Rock's long-awaited return finally arrived. The Rock's partner, John Cena, and their opponents, The Miz and R-Truth, were already by the ring when he entered the arena. The Rock stood high up on the **turnbuckle** and saluted his fans. The crowd cheered loudly for their returning hero.

The Rock stands on the turnbuckle before a match.

When the opening bell rang, The Rock grabbed The Miz in a **headlock** and then sent him flying to the ground with a shoulder block. To help his fallen partner, R-Truth jumped in. Seconds later, The Rock hurled R-Truth over the top rope and out of the ring. The Rock had quickly shown that even after seven years of not wrestling, he still was a superstar in the ring.

The Miz is one of the toughest tag team performers in the WWE. He is a four-time tag team champion.

The Rock (right) performing a move called the Rock Bottom on R-Truth

Still the Best

The Rock was unstoppable, but later, after he **tagged out**, his partner got into trouble. The Miz pummeled John Cena with a few different moves. Then R-Truth joined in for an illegal double team attack. The Rock tagged back in and stunned The Miz and then R-Truth with a lightning-fast flurry of blows, causing R-Truth to roll out of the ring. The Rock then turned to The Miz and put him in a Sharpshooter.

The Miz (right) battles against John Cena (left) during a match in 2009.

In a tag team match, only one wrestler from a team is allowed to face an opponent at a time. Double team attacks—in which both members of a team take on an opponent at the same time—are against the rules.

The Miz fought back, but The Rock would not be stopped. He dropped The Miz to the canvas with a devastating **Spinebuster** and then gave him the **People's Elbow**. The Miz was done and the match was over. The Rock's team had won!

The Rock prepares to give The Miz the People's Elbow.

Many Sides of The Rock

On April 1, 2012, The Rock returned to one-on-one wrestling, defeating former partner John Cena, and leaving no doubt that inside the ring, he's still the world's toughest wrestler. Outside the ring, however, is a different story. People are sometimes surprised to learn that The Rock is friendly and gentle. That's because wrestling isn't all that he learned from his dad. "I taught my son that when he's inside the ring, he's The Rock, and anything goes," said Rocky Johnson, "but outside the ring he's Dwayne Johnson—and to always remember that."

The Rock after defeating John Cena

The Rock wrestling against John Cena was the main event at WrestleMania XXVIII (28) in Miami, Florida, on April 1, 2012. It was a furious battle, but in the end, The Rock won the match.

Dwayne "The Rock" Johnson has many different sides. To his WWE fans, his role as world's greatest wrestler will always be the most important.

The Rock with some of his young fans

The Rock File

Stats:

Born:	May 2, 1972, Hayward, California
Height:	6′ 5″ (1.96 m)
Weight:	260 pounds (118 kg)
Greatest Moves:	Sharpshooter, People's Elbow, Rock Bottom

Fun Facts:

- In his spare time, The Rock loves watching cartoons, playing video games, and singing.
- At the University of Miami, The Rock earned his college degree in criminology, which is the study of how criminals act.
- The Rock's return to one-on-one wrestling drew a crowd of more than 78,000 people, the most people ever to attend an event at Sun Life Stadium in Miami, Florida.

The Rock puts John Cena in a headlock during WrestleMania XXVIII (28).

Glossary

Canadian Football League (kuh-NAY-dee-uhn FUT-*bal* LEEG) the professional football league of Canada

dominant (DOM-uh-nuhnt) the most powerful; the very best

duo (DOO-oh) a pair, a team of two

fury (FYOO-ree) an incredible force

headlock (HED-lok) a hold in which a wrestler tightly grips an arm around an opponent's head

Intercontinental Championship (*in*-tur-*kon*-tuh-NEN-tuhl CHAM-pee-uhn-*ship*) one of the WWE's wrestling titles; a wrestler often competes for this title before wrestling for one of the WWE's bigger titles

opposing (uh-POHZ-ing) competing against another person or team

People's Elbow (PEE-puhlz EL-boh) a move often used by The Rock to finish a match; The Rock crisscrosses the ring, then drops onto his fallen opponent, landing his elbow on his opponent's ribs

ring names (RING NAYMZ) the names that wrestlers use while in the ring; usually not the wrestlers' real names

roles (ROHLZ) acting parts

Sharpshooter (SHARP-*shoot*-ur) a wrestling hold in which one wrestler presses his or her opponent's face down against the floor while holding on to both of the opponent's legs; the move creates pain in the opponent's back

Spinebuster (SPINE-buhs-tur) a move in which a wrestler faces an opponent, grabs the opponent around the legs, lifts the opponent up, and slams the opponent down onto his or her back

tagged out (TAGD OUT) when the active wrestler in a tag team match slaps hands with his or her partner, leaving the ring and allowing the partner to take over

tag team (TAG TEEM) a wrestling event in which two-person teams of wrestlers battle each other; usually only one wrestler from each team is allowed in the ring at a time and teammates switch places inside and outside the ring by "tagging" or hand-slapping each other

technique (tek-NEEK) a way of doing something

title (TYE-tuhl) the championship

turnbuckle (TURN-buhk-uhl) the device that connects the ropes in each corner of a wrestling ring

villainous (VIL-uhn-uhss) very evil

WWE (DUHB-*uhl*-yoo DUHB-*uhl*-yoo EE) the main pro wrestling organization in the United States

WWE Championship (DUHB-*uhl*-yoo DUHB-*uhl*-yoo EE CHAM-pee-uhn-*ship*) one of the WWE's most important titles, along with the World Heavyweight Championship

Bibliography

Hughes, Zondra. "The Rock Talks About Race, Wrestling And Women." *Ebony* (July 2001).

The Rock with Joe Layden. *The Rock Says . . . The Most Electrifying Man in Sports-Entertainment.* New York: Avon Books (2000).

WWE.com

Read More

Gorman, Jacqueline Laks. *Dwayne "The Rock" Johnson.* Pleasantville, NY: Gareth Stevens (2008).

Orr, Tamra. *Day by Day with Dwayne "The Rock" Johnson.* Hockessin, DE: Mitchell Lane (2012).

West, Tracey. *Race to the Rumble #1.* New York: Grosset & Dunlap (2011).

Learn More Online

To learn more about The Rock , visit
www.bearportpublishing.com/WrestlingsToughGuys

Index